HOW NOT TO DIE

(PLANT BASED) DIET COOKBOOK:

Recipes to Help Give You a Prolonged Healthy Lifestyle Free From Disease.

By

STEVE COLLINS

Copyright © 2019, By: *STEVE COLLINS*

ISBN-13: 978-1-950772-29-2
ISBN-10: 1-950772-29-2

All Rights Reserved. No part of this publication may be reproduced in any form or by any means, including scanning, photocopying, or otherwise without prior written permission of the copyright holder.

Disclaimer:

The information provided in this book is designed to provide helpful information on the subjects discussed. The publisher and author are not responsible for any specific health or allergy needs that may require medical supervision and are not liable for any damages or negative consequences from any treatment, action, application or preparation, to any person reading or following the information in this book.

Table of Contents

INTRODUCTION TO THE PLANT BASE DIET FOR A HEALTHY LIFESTYLE 7

THE PLANT BASE RECIPE FOR A DISEASE FREE SOCIETY 9

    PLANT BASE BREAKFAST RECIPES 9

        Power Porridge 9

        Low Fat Cinnamon Nut Granola 11

        Oat and Quinoa Cereal 13

        Heart-Healthy Oatmeal 14

        Baked Pears with Cardamom 15

        Green Berry Smoothie 16

        Carrot Pancakes 17

        Sweet Potato Hash Browns 19

        Heart Healthy Smoothie 20

        Cornmeal Waffles 21

        Buckwheat Pancakes 23

        Pumpkin Spice Chia Pudding 25

        Healing Turmeric Smoothie 27

        Homemade Almond Milk 28

        Muesli 29

        Pumpkin Pancakes 30

        Groovy Green Smoothie Ingredients: 32

        Tofu Scramble 33

        Potato Pancakes 34

        No Oil Roasted Potatoes 35

    PLANT BASE APPETIZER AND SNACKS 36

        Healthy Onion Dip 36

        Oil-Free Potato, Yam or Tortilla Chips 37

- Bitchin' Sauce Original Recipe 38
- Basil Spinach Dip 39
- Mango Salsa 40
- Baked Tortilla Chips 41
- Sun-dried Tomato, Basil Hummus 42
- Baked Corn Casserole with Spinach & Chilies 43
- Baby Lima Bean Hummus 45
- Baked Artichoke Dip 46
- Low-Fat Hummus 48
- Edam me Dip 49
- Roasted Carrot and Garlic Hummus 50
- Roasted Red Pepper Dip 52

PLANT BASE SOUP AND SALAD RECIPES 53

- Creamy Curried Cauliflower Soup 53
- Curried Coconut Lentil Yam Soup 55
- Moroccan Stew with Kale 56

Hearty Vegetable Soup 58

- Mushroom Quinoa Soup 59
- **Vegetable Soup with Ravioli** 61
- **Avocado, Papaya Gazpacho** 63
- **Tomato, Carrot, Brussels Sprout Soup** 64
- **Lentil Pea Soup** 66
- **Roasted Tomato Bisque** 68
- **Thai Carrot Soup** 70
- **Roasted Cauliflower Soup** 72
- **Cold Cucumber Soup** 74
- Tomato Coconut Curry Soup 75
- **Curried Chickpea Rice Salad** 77
- **Roasted Cauliflower and Mushroom Salad** 79

Kale Salad with Oranges ... 80
Roasted Potato & Green Bean Salad ... 81
Roasted Yam, Onion and Mushroom Salad ... 82
Corn, Tomato, Avocado Salad ... 83
Quinoa Salad with Spicy Peanut Dressing ... 85

PLANT BASED DESSERT RECIPES ... 87
Pumpkin Spice Chia Pudding ... 87
Baked Pears with Cardamom ... 89
Raspberry Jell-O ... 90
Green Berry Smoothie ... 92
Chocolate Chip Chickpea Cookies ... 93
Groovy Green Smoothie ... 95
Homemade Soy Yogurt ... 96
Strawberry Ice Cream ... 97
Black Bean Brownies ... 98
Blueberry Lemon Coconut Bars ... 100
Carrot Pudding with Indian Spices ... 102

PLANT BASED MAIN DISH RECIPES ... 104
Sweet and Sour Tofu ... 104
Broccoli Cauliflower Veggie Divan ... 106
Moroccan Stew with Kale ... 108
Thai Curried Potatoes with Chard ... 110
Pasta with Spinach Marinara Sauce ... 111
Falafel Burger ... 112
Vegetarian Chili ... 114
Asian Noodle Salad ... 116
Lightly Curried Vegetable Wraps ... 118
Mushrooms with Burgundy Sauce Over Polenta ... 120
Baked Corn Casserole with Spinach & Chilies ... 122

Baked Tofu 124

Eggplant Szechuan-Style with Peppers & Mushrooms 126

Pasta with Pesto (No Added Oil) 127

Chili Topped Potatoes with Corn Salsa 128

Veggie Tacos 130

Stuffed Peppers 132

Beet, Black Bean Burger 134

Thai Coconut Curry Tofu 136

Tempeh in Hearty Mushroom-Lager Sauce 138

CONCLUSION 140

INTRODUCTION TO THE PLANT BASE DIET FOR A HEALTHY LIFESTYLE

How Not To Die "A new way of looking at nutrition and health reveals the groundbreaking scientific evidence behind the only diet that can prevent and reverse many of the causes of premature death and disability in our society. It went further to also show how the right nutrition prevents disease and transforms our genes so we can live healthier, longer.

This plague that causes premature deaths in our society can be prevented through simple changes in diet and lifestyle. Dr. Michael Greger, the internationally-renowned nutrition expert, physician, and founder of NutritionFacts.org, in his book "HOW NOT TO DIE" examines the fifteen top causes of premature death in America-heart disease, various cancers, diabetes, Parkinson's, high blood pressure, and more-and explains how nutritional and lifestyle interventions can sometimes trump prescription pills and other pharmaceutical and surgical approaches, freeing us to live healthier lives.

However, most doctors are good at treating acute illnesses but bad at preventing chronic disease. The fifteen leading causes of death as outlined by Dr. Michael Greger, is known to have claim the lives of 1.6 million Americans annually.

The sole purpose of this book is in accordance to the advice of Dr. Michael Greger, all of it backed up by strong scientific evidence, you will learn which foods to eat and which lifestyle changes to make to live longer.

It high time you put down that glass of milk and add flaxseed to your diet whenever you can, switch to a whole-food, plant-based diet, which has been repeatedly shown not just to prevent the disease but often stop it in its tracks.

Finally, in addition to showing what to eat to help treat the top fifteen causes of death, this cookbook includes Dr. Greger's Daily Dozens of foods that you are to consume daily to live longer, healthier lives.

THE PLANT BASE RECIPE FOR A DISEASE FREE SOCIETY

PLANT BASE BREAKFAST RECIPES

Power Porridge

Ingredients:

1 Tablespoon of lentils

2 Tablespoon of oat bran

1 Tablespoon of flax seeds, ground

1 Tablespoon of sunflower seeds

1 Tablespoon of pumpkin seeds, raw

1 Tablespoon of raisins

Sweeten if you need to with honey or preferably maple syrup or try the new sweetener Monk Fruit

2 cups of almond or oat milk

2 Tablespoons of steel cut oats

1 Tablespoon of Kasha (buckwheat grouts, toasted)

1 Tablespoon of chia seeds

2 Tablespoons of walnuts (rough chopped)

4 large dates (rough chopped)

Fresh or better still frozen berries and/or bananas

Directions:

1. First, you heat almond or oat milk to a boil add lentils, then add grains, seeds and oats stir, turn down the heat to simmer, stirring occasionally.
2. After which you simmer for about fifteen minutes until the lentils are tender (**NOTE:** feel free to add more almond milk to keep the consistency creamy).
3. After that, you add the nuts and dried fruit, stir and cover to simmer only until the dried fruits have warmed.
4. Then you cut fresh fruit to add on top.
5. Finally, you put in a bowl then drizzle honey over all.

Low Fat Cinnamon Nut Granola

Ingredients:

Serves 4

2 cups of puffed corn

½ cup of sliced almonds, walnuts or better still pistachios

½ cup of unsweetened apple sauce

1 dropper full of Stevia liquid sweetener (it is optional)

1 teaspoon of vanilla

½ cup of shredded coconut (it is optional)

2 cups of whole oats

2 cups, puffed millet

¾ cup of dried cranberries or better still raisins

¼ cup of honey / maple syrup

2 teaspoons of cinnamon

Dash of salt

Directions:

1. Meanwhile, you heat oven to 300 degrees.
2. After which you measure oats, puffed corn and millet into a large bowl and add nuts.
3. After that, in a small bowl, add applesauce, honey or maple syrup, cinnamon, vanilla and salt and mix well.
4. Then you add liquid ingredients to the cereals and stir to combine.

5. At this point, you spread on two baking sheets covered with parchment paper.
6. This is when you bake for 30-45 minutes turning every 15 minutes until lightly browned.
7. Finally, you add dried fruit (and shredded coconut if using) and stir.

Oat and Quinoa Cereal

Ingredients:

1/3 teaspoon of cinnamon

¼ teaspoon of salt

1/3 cup of quinoa flakes

½ cup of frozen berries (defrosted)

2 cups of water

1/3 teaspoon of vanilla extract

½ cup of rolled oats

1/3 cup of plain yogurt

3 teaspoons of honey

Directions:

1. First, you add water to saucepan along with the oats, quinoa, cinnamon, vanilla and salt.
2. After which you bring to a boil, lower the heat and cook until thickened.
3. Then you serve in a bowl along with half of the yogurt, half of the berries and a drizzle of honey.
4. Enjoy

Heart-Healthy Oatmeal

Ingredients:

1 ½ cups of water

1 Tablespoon of chia seeds

¼ cup of walnuts or better still mixed nuts

¾ cup of old-fashioned organic oats

2 Tablespoons of ground flaxseeds

¼ teaspoon of salt

1 cup of organic berries (I often used frozen)

Directions:

1. First, you bring 1 ½ cups water, oatmeal, ground flax, chia seeds, and salt to a boil.
2. After which you turn down the heat and simmer for about 7-10 minutes until the water evaporated and the oatmeal soft.
3. After that, you chop berries into bite-sized pieces.
4. Finally, you serve oatmeal topped with the berries and nuts with soy yogurt or nut milk.

Baked Pears with Cardamom

Ingredients:

½ teaspoon of ground cardamom

2-4 firm ripe pears (halved and seeded)

2 Tablespoons of sugar

¼ cup of white wine

1 teaspoon of vanilla

1 ½ Tablespoons of lemon juice

Directions:

1. Meanwhile, you heat oven to 400 degrees F.
2. After which you combine wine, cardamom and vanilla in 8" square baking dish.
3. After that, you place pears cut-side up in baking dish and pour lemon juice over.
4. At this point, you sprinkle with sugar.
5. Then you cover pan with foil, place on the middle rack in the oven, and bake 30 minutes, or until tender.
6. This is when you remove foil and move pan to top rack.
7. Furthermore, you broil 5 minutes, or until lightly browned (NOTE: Watch carefully).
8. Finally, you transfer pears to a serving plate and drizzle with juice from the pan.

Green Berry Smoothie

Ingredients:

1 cup of your favorite non-dairy drink (I prefer hemp or almond milk)

Fiber and / or better still powdered greens (it is optional)

1 cups of frozen berries (**NOTE:** any mix - organic strawberries, blueberries, cranberries are my favorite)

½ cup of water for thinning

1-2 leaves of Swiss chard broken into smaller bits

Directions:

1. First, you add the berries, Swiss chard and on-dairy drink to the blender.
2. After which you wait until smooth, adding water to thick to the consistency you like.
3. After that, you add any fiber, powdered greens or protein powder of your choice and wait just a few more seconds.

Carrot Pancakes
Makes about 12 small pancakes
Ingredients:

½ cup of whole wheat flour (or better still gluten-free flour)

½ teaspoon of salt

1 teaspoon of baking soda

1 Tablespoon of ground flax seeds or better still 1 Tablespoon of Chia seeds (optional)

½ banana (mashed)

Maple syrup or better still applesauce

1 cup of old fashioned oats

¼ cup of cornmeal

1 teaspoon of cinnamon

1 teaspoon of baking powder

1 large carrot (peeled and grated)

1 teaspoon of vanilla extract

1 cup of almond or better still soy milk

DIRECTIONS:

1. First, you mix all of the dry ingredients in a large bowl.
2. After which you add the grated carrot and stir.
3. After that, you add the wet ingredients to the dry ingredients in the bowl: almond or soy milk, vanilla, and mashed banana.
4. Then you stir to combine well.
5. At this point, you let sit about 5 minutes (NOTE: If the mixture is too thick, I suggest you add more of your liquid).

6. Furthermore, you heat a nonstick pan (NOTE: If you're using a metal pan, I suggest you'll need to spray on a little oil).
7. Then when the pan is heated to medium, drop large spoonsful of the pancake mix onto it and cook until lightly browned on the bottom.
8. At this point, you flip and cook on the other side.
9. Finally, you serve with maple syrup and / or applesauce and the rest of the banana sliced or blueberries.

Sweet Potato Hash Browns

Ingredients:

1 large onion (chopped)

½ teaspoon of Smokey paprika (it is optional)

Pepper to taste

2 large sweet potatoes or yams (chopped)

1 large red or better still green pepper (chopped)

½ teaspoon of salt or to taste

Directions:

1. Meanwhile, you heat a large nonstick skillet and add the onions.
2. After which you cook until they start to brown slightly.
3. After that, you add the pepper, potatoes and spices and continue to cook, turning frequently so as not to burn.
4. Furthermore, if you need to, add a little water and cover to help the cooking process, but make sure you uncover and let the water evaporate before serving.
5. Finally, salt and pepper to taste.

Heart Healthy Smoothie

Ingredients:

¼ cup of old fashioned oatmeal

2 large leaves romaine lettuce or better still a handful of other greens like kale or spinach

¼ pomegranate juice

½ -1 cup of mixed frozen organic berries like cranberries, blueberries and strawberries.

1 Tablespoon of flaxseeds

¾ cup of soy milk (I prefer the West soy sugar-free brand, cuss it only has beans and water.)

Directions:

1. First, you add all of the ingredients to a blender and blend until smooth.
2. After that, you add more water if you'd like it a little thinner.

Cornmeal Waffles

Ingredients:

½ cup of oats

1 ½ teaspoons of baking powder

1 teaspoon of cinnamon

1/3 cup of applesauce

1 Tablespoon of coconut oil (optional)

1 cup of blueberries

2/3 cup of chopped walnuts

1 cup of cornmeal

2/3 cup of whole wheat flour (for gluten-free, I suggest you use 1/3 buckwheat flour + GF flour or 2/3 GF flour)

½ teaspoon of salt.

1 ½ cup of almond or better still soy milk (or other nut milk)

1 Tablespoon of maple syrup

1 ½ teaspoons of vanilla extract

Maple syrup

Directions:

1. First, you mix the wet ingredients, milk, applesauce, maple syrup, and vanilla extract in a bowl.
2. After which in a separate bowl mix the dry ingredients, cornmeal, oats, and flour, baking powder, salt and cinnamon.

3. After that, you pour the dry ingredients into the wet and combine carefully.
4. Then you cook in your waffle maker according to the directions.

Directions on how to make blueberry syrup:

1. First, you pour a little maple syrup over the cup of blueberries and warm a few seconds in the microwave.
2. Then you top each waffle with a dollop of applesauce, the blueberry/maple syrup mix and a few walnuts.

Buckwheat Pancakes

Ingredients:

½ cup of cornmeal

1 teaspoon of baking soda

½ teaspoon of salt (or to taste)

1 to 1 ½ cups of non-dairy milk

½ cup of applesauce

1 Tablespoon of maple syrup (optional)

1 cup of blueberries (frozen or fresh)

1 cup of buckwheat flour

½ cup of oatmeal

1 teaspoon of baking powder

1 teaspoon of cinnamon

½ large banana or better still 1 whole small (frozen or fresh)

1 teaspoon of vanilla

½ cup of chopped walnuts or better still mixed nuts

Directions:

1. First, you mix all of the dry ingredients, buckwheat through cinnamon.
2. After which you mix the wet ingredients in a separate bowl, non-dairy milk through maple syrup. (Note: make sure you defrost frozen banana in the microwave first.)

3. After that, you pour the wet ingredients into the dry and mix until just combined.
4. Then you let sit for a minute.
5. At this point, you add a little more non-dairy milk if it's too thick.
6. Furthermore, you heat a non-stick pan (add a little oil spray to a metal pan if using) and drop about 2 large spoonsful of batter onto the pan.
7. After that, you flip when edges seem dry.
8. Make sure you don't overcook, because it can lead to dryness.
9. Finally, you remove to a plate and serve with blueberries, sliced banana, maple syrup (or more applesauce) and nuts.

Pumpkin Spice Chia Pudding

Ingredients:

1 cup of organic pumpkin puree

1 teaspoon of vanilla extract

½ cup of chia seeds found in most health food stores.

2 cups of unsweetened organic almond milk

2 Tablespoons of almond butter

¼ cup of maple syrup or better still honey (please see note below: to cut down on the sugar, use 1 teaspoon of liquid Stevia)

2 teaspoons of pumpkin spice (or better still use 1 teaspoon of cinnamon, ¼ teaspoon of ginger, pinch ground clove, pinch allspice. (NOTE: The recipe didn't call for it but you could also add ¼ teaspoon of cardamom if you're adventurous.)

Optional toppings: *chopped walnuts or pecans, pumpkin seeds, shredded coconut or small chocolate chips.*

DIRECTIONS:

1. First, you pour 1 cup of almond milk into a glass bowl and add pumpkin puree.
2. After which you whisk until the puree is completely dissolved.
3. After that, you add the almond butter, vanilla, maple syrup and pumpkin spice and whisk till incorporated.
4. At this point, you add remaining almond milk and begin adding the chia seeds, whisking to mix.

5. Furthermore, you let stand for 5 minutes and then whisk to incorporate the chia seeds throughout the pudding.
6. After that, you place in the refrigerator for 15 minutes then remove and whisk again.
7. Finally, you chill in the fridge for about 30 minutes to allow the pudding to set.

Note: If you using Stevia, I suggest you start with about 1/3 teaspoon and work up to the sweetness you like.

Healing Turmeric Smoothie

tips:

However, this smoothie has an unusual ingredient beside the turmeric--black pepper, because it enhances the effect of turmeric.

Ingredients:

2 frozen bananas (broken into pieces)

1 teaspoon of ground turmeric (**NOTE:** start with less and add more to taste) or better still use ½ inch fresh, peeled and grated

¼ teaspoon of vanilla extract

A pinch or twist from the pepper mill

2 cups of non-dairy milk such as almond, soy or better still coconut

1 cup of frozen mango or other fruit

1 Tablespoon of hemp, flax or chia seeds

¼ teaspoon of ground cinnamon

Directions:

1. First, you place all of the ingredients into a high-powered blender.
2. Then you blend until smooth, scraping the sides as necessary.

Homemade Almond Milk

Ingredients:

4 cups of filtered water

2 dates (coarsely chopped)

1 cup of raw almonds, soaked in water to cover for several hours or better still overnight.

1 teaspoon of vanilla

2 pinches of salt

Directions:

1. First, you add almonds, 4 cups water, salt, vanilla and dates to your high powered blender.
2. After which you cover securely and blend slowly at first.
3. After that, you then turn up the speed too high for about 30 seconds or until well blended.
4. At this point, you pour the blended mixture into a nut-bag or cheesecloth and massage with your hand to extract all of the liquid.
5. Then you discard the left-over pulp or save for another use such as in baked items.
6. Finally, you pour into your container and chill.

Muesli

Ingredients:

1 cup of wheat flakes (Uncle Sam Brand)

½ cup of hemp hearts

½ cup of slivered almonds or better still whole almonds, sliced

½ cup of walnuts

½ cup of raisins or better still other dried fruit (raisins have no sugar)

1 teaspoon of almond extract

2 cups of old fashioned oats

1 cup of quinoa Flakes (found near the hot cereals)

½ cup of ground flax seeds

½ cup of raw pumpkin seeds

½ cup of coconut flakes

1 teaspoon of cinnamon

Directions:

1. First, you place all of the ingredients in a large bowl and stir to combine.
2. After which you store in a glass jar or container with a tight lid.
3. Then you serve with soy yogurt, berries and non-dairy milk.

Pumpkin Pancakes

Ingredients:

¼ cup of cornmeal

2 teaspoons of baking powder

½ teaspoon of salt

1 teaspoon of ground cinnamon

½ teaspoon of allspice

1 ½ cup of non-dairy milk

½ cup of oatmeal

1 ¼ of cup whole wheat flour (Gluten Free version)

1 teaspoon of baking soda

½ cup of pumpkin puree (canned)

½ teaspoon of ground ginger

1 teaspoon of vanilla extract

1 large or 2 small ripe banana (mashed)

Directions:

1. Meanwhile, you heat griddle to medium.
2. After which you place all of the dry ingredients in a large bowl and stir to combine.
3. After that, you mix the wet ingredients, banana, pumpkin, vanilla, and non-dairy milk, in a separate bowl and whisk.

4. At this point, you combine the wet and dry ingredients until just moist.
5. Then you lightly spray your griddle with oil and drop the batter by large spoonful's onto it.
6. Furthermore, you cook until bubbles start to form around the edges and the bottom is nicely browned.
7. After that, you flip and cook the other side.
8. Finally, you serve with maple syrup or jam and your favorite fruit and / or nuts.

For a Gluten-Free Version: I suggest you up the oats to ¾ cup and Substitute 1 cup of gluten-free flour for the whole wheat flour.

Groovy Green Smoothie

Ingredients:

1 orange peeled into sections

½ scoop of Super Seed

1 cup of frozen organic berries

3 romaine lettuce leaves

¾ cup of almond milk

Directions:

1. First, you put all into blender except the Super Seed.
2. After which you blend until smooth.
3. After that, you add a little water if too thick.
4. Then you pour in the Super Seed and wait just a few seconds.

Tofu Scramble

Ingredients:

1 onion (roughly chopped)

½ to 1 8 oz. of carton mushrooms, sliced

Salt and pepper (to taste)

1 package firm tofu (drained and crumbled)

1 red pepper (roughly chopped)

½ teaspoon of turmeric

½ teaspoon of curry power

Directions:

1. First, you sauté all of the vegetables in a small amount of water in non-stick pan.
2. Then when veggies are soft, add the crumbled tofu, spices and salt and pepper and stir to combine.
3. Remember the mixture should turn yellow from the spices and begin to look like eggs.
4. After that, you continue to cook until most of moisture from the tofu has cooked off and it's heated through, stirring frequently so as not to stick.

Potato Pancakes

Ingredients:

¼ minced onion (or better still grated)

Add about 1 teaspoon of any herbs or spices you like such as parsley, chives, or curry.

Salt and pepper to taste

2 cups of mashed potatoes (our had chives in them already)

¼ Flour (make sure you use anything you have, oat, whole wheat, buckwheat…)

Directions:

1. First, you mix all of the ingredients in a large bowl.
2. After which you heat a large skillet and use a little oil or spray to prevent sticking (**NOTE**: a non-stick pan really helps).
3. After that, you drop by large spoonsful onto the hot pan and spread a little with your spoon and fingers.
4. Then you flip when browned on one side for about 2-3 min.
5. At this point, you flatten more with your spatula and cook until browned on the second side.
6. Finally, you serve with applesauce, maple syrup or blueberries.

No Oil Roasted Potatoes

Ingredients:

1 pepper (preferably any color, cut into 1" pieces)

Salt and Pepper

2 russet potatoes and 2 yams (peeled and cut into 1" pieces).

1 red onion (cut into 1" pieces)

2-3 Tablespoons of flour

Directions:

1. Meanwhile, you heat the oven to 450 degrees F.
2. After which you place the potatoes, onion and peppers in a large sauté pan with a little water and once water is boiling, steam for about 5 minutes until the potatoes are crisp tender.
3. After that, you drain the potatoes, return the pieces to the pot (NOTE: don't put the pot back on the heat), and sprinkle the flour over.
4. At this point, you put the lid back on the pot, and shake it vigorously for a few seconds. However, you are marring the edges, which will facilitate the crunchiness of the potatoes later on.
5. Then you dump the potatoes onto a sheet pan lightly sprayed with oil and make sure they are in a single layer (NOTE: remember don't crowd the potatoes, or the edges won't get crispy).
6. This is when you sprinkle with salt and pepper to taste.
7. Finally, you roast for 30-45 minutes at 450 degrees F, turning after half way done, but watch them carefully so as not to burn.

PLANT BASE APPETIZER AND SNACKS
Healthy Onion Dip

Ingredients:

½ onion (sliced thinly)

Juice from 1 lemon

2 Tablespoons of dried chopped onion (see below)

½ block (about 14 oz.) firm organic tofu

2 cloves garlic (roughly chopped)

2 Tablespoons of apple cider vinegar

2 Tablespoons of white miso

Directions:

1. First, you dry-sauté the onions in a non-stick pan (no water) until lightly browned, turning frequently.
2. After which you add garlic at the end of the onion browning and sauté for a few minutes.
3. After that, you set aside to cool.
4. At this point, you add the tofu, lemon, miso, apple cider vinegar and cooled onion mixture to a food processor.
5. Then you process until smooth and remove to a bowl.
6. Furthermore, you add the dried chopped onion and mix to combine.
7. After that, you cool in refrigerator for about an hour so flavors can blend.
8. Finally, you serve with oil-free potato, yam or tortilla chips, crackers or veggie sticks.

Oil-Free Potato, Yam or Tortilla Chips

Ingredients:

Potatoes or Yams, 2-3 sliced thinly by hand or better still with a mandolin.

Corn tortillas, 12 count, cut into 6 triangles (I prefer Food for Life's Sprouted Corn Tortillas)

Salt

Directions:
Oven:

1. Meanwhile, you heat oven to 390 degrees
2. After which you place in a single layer on a baking sheet lined with parchment paper or sprayed with a little oil.
3. After that, you sprinkle or spray a small amount of water over the chips and lightly salt.
4. At this point, you bake for 8-10 minutes, flip them over and then cook again for about 5-10 minute.
5. Remember that the regular potatoes will take less time.

NOTE: make sure you watch them carefully as they're easy to overcook.

Microwave:

1. **First, you p**lace in a single layer on a plate or use the handy microwavable gadget below.
2. Then you microwave for about 4 minutes or until crisp.

Bitchin' Sauce Original Recipe

Ingredients:

½ cup of water

2 cloves of garlic

2 teaspoons of Bragg's liquid aminos or low-sodium tamari

¼ teaspoon of salt

¼ teaspoon Smokey (or better still regular) paprika

¾ cup of raw almonds

1/3 cup of fresh lemon juice

¼ cup of onion (chopped)

1 teaspoon of cider vinegar

¼ teaspoon of cumin

¼ teaspoon of coriander

Directions:

1. First, you place all of the ingredients in a high-powdered blender.
2. After which you slowly blend for one minute.
3. After that, you turn the dial up to high and continue to blend until smooth and creamy.
4. At this point, you store in the refrigerator (NOTE: The sauce may separate, but stir it if it does).
5. Make sure you increase the water if you'd like it to be saucier.

Basil Spinach Dip

Ingredients:

1 (10 package) of frozen spinach, defrosted

¼ cup of apple cider vinegar

2 Tablespoons of light miso

½ teaspoon of onion powder

1 can water chestnuts (drained)

One block of tofu, drained and pressed (optional – remember that it'll be a little looser if you don't press)

1 cup packed basil leaves

1 Tablespoon of spicy mustard

½ teaspoon of granulated garlic

2 Tablespoons of nutritional yeast (it is optional)

Directions:

1. First, in a food processor, blend tofu, apple cider vinegar, mustard, onion powder, granulated garlic, miso and nutritional yeast on high until well blended.
2. After which you squeeze the water out of the spinach and add to the bowl of the food processor along with the water chestnuts.
3. After that, you pulse a few times to break up the water chestnuts leaving some chunkiness.
4. Finally, you chill for a few hours and serve with veggies or baked tortilla chips.

Mango Salsa

Ingredients:

½ cup of peeled, diced cucumber

1/3 cup of diced red pepper

1 tablespoon of lime juice

Salt and pepper

1 mango (peeled and diced)

1 tablespoon of jalapeno, finely chopped

1/3 cup of diced red onion

1/3 cup of roughly chopped cilantro leaves

Directions:

1. First, you combine the mango, cucumber, jalapeño, red onion, lime juice and cilantro and mix well.
2. Then you season with salt and pepper to taste.

Baked Tortilla Chips
Makes 72 chips
Ingredients:

Corn tortillas, 12 count, cut into 6 triangles (I prefer Food for Life's Sprouted Corn Tortillas)

Salt

Directions:
Oven:

1. Meanwhile, you heat oven to 390 degrees
2. After which you place in a single layer on a baking sheet.
3. After that, you sprinkle or spray a small amount of water over the chips and lightly salt.
4. Then you bake for about 8-10 minutes (NOTE: Watch them carefully as they're easy to overcook).

Microwave:

1. First, you place in a single layer on a plate.
2. Then you microwave for about 4 minutes or until crisp.

Sun-dried Tomato, Basil Hummus
Serves 6
Ingredients:

2 cloves garlic (roughly chopped)

1 cup of basil leaves

2 Tablespoons of tahini (it is found near the peanut butters in the store)

Salt to taste

1 can of garbanzo beans (chickpeas)

Juice from 2 lemons

1/3 cup of sun-dried tomatoes packed in oil

5-7 shakes of Tabasco sauce

Small amount of water

Directions:

1. First, you rinse the sun-dried tomatoes in a strainer under hot water to remove most of the oil.
2. After which you add all of the ingredients into the bowl of a food processor.
3. After that, you pulse a few times to combine and then stir mixture with a spatula.
4. Then you continue to run processor, adding a little water to a consistency you like.
5. Finally, you serve with a side of raw vegetables or crackers.

Baked Corn Casserole with Spinach & Chilies

Serves 5-6
Ingredients:

1 cup cornmeal

¾ cup of milk alternative like almond

2 cans of diced mild chilies

2 ears fresh corn, taken off of cob, or better still pkg frozen, thawed

½ teaspoon of cumin

½ teaspoon of cayenne pepper

1 (14-16 oz.) block of firm tofu

1 ½ cup of water

1 pkg of frozen spinach (thawed and water squeezed out)

3 cloves garlic (minced)

1 teaspoon of baking powder

1 teaspoon of Salt & Pepper to taste

Condiments: Store-bought Salsa or better still Enchilada sauce

Directions:

1. Meanwhile, you heat oven to 400 degrees.
2. After which you prepare cornmeal by heating 1 ½ cup water in a medium saucepan with ½ cup of the milk alternative until almost boiling.
3. After that, you slowly whisk in the corn meal and stir constantly until mixture thickens.

4. At this point, you transfer to a large bowl.
5. To a food processor, you add the garlic, tofu, 1 cup corn and remaining ¼ cup milk alternative.
6. Then you process until smooth.
7. Furthermore, you stir into the cooked cornmeal in the large bowl.
8. After that, you add the spinach, remaining whole corn, diced chilies, baking powder, spices, salt and pepper and mix well (NOTE: This may take some elbow grease).
9. Then you bake for 60-70 minutes until crispy and firm at the edges.
10. Remember, the middle will be a bit wiggly still.
11. Let stand for about 20-30 minutes before serving.
12. Finally, you serve topped with salsa or enchilada sauce

Baby Lima Bean Hummus

Ingredients:

Make about 2 cups

½ cup of cilantro

¼ cup of lemon juice

2-3 of cloves garlic

1/8 cup of water (as needed)

1 bag of frozen baby lima beans (cooked according to directions)

2 Tablespoons of red miso

1 tablespoon of tahini

5 shakes of Tabasco sauce

Directions:

1. First, you place all of the ingredients in the bowl of a food processor and process.
2. After which you stop and scrape down the sides to incorporate all.
3. After that, you add water to thin as needed.
4. Then you serve with sliced apples, vegetables or whole grain crackers.

Baked Artichoke Dip

Serves 5-6
Ingredients:

1 cup of cooked red or better still Yukon gold potatoes, packed

2 Tablespoons of apple cider vinegar

2 teaspoons of salt

½ teaspoon of freshly ground black pepper

3 Tablespoons of fresh (flat-leaf parsley)

4-5 oz. of spinach, you can use frozen, thawed and drained

½ cup of raw cashews

4 Tablespoons of freshly squeezed lemon juice

4 cloves garlic (minced)

4 Tablespoons of nutritional yeast

1 ¾ cup of nondairy milk (soy milk is best for creaminess)

1 (14-oz) can or jarred artichoke hearts (drained, rinsed)

¼ cup of fresh basil leaves (packed)

Directions:

1. Meanwhile, you heat the oven to 375°F.
2. After which you place the cashews in a food processor and blend until finely ground.
3. After that, you scrape down the sides of the processor bowl and add the potatoes, lemon juice, vinegar, and garlic, the nutritional yeast, salt, and the pepper.

4. Then you pulse a few times.
5. At this point, you add ½ cup nondairy milk and purée until smooth.
6. This is when you add the remaining milk and the parsley.
7. Furthermore, you purée until very smooth and well combined, scraping down the sides of the bowl when necessary.
8. After that, you add the artichoke, basil, and spinach and pulse lightly to incorporate the ingredients while retaining a slightly chunky consistency (NOTE: it will be pretty running, but will firm up after baking).
9. After which you pour into a medium-size baking dish and bake, uncovered, for 25 to 30 minutes.
10. Finally, you remove and let cool for about 5 minutes before serving.

Low-Fat Hummus

Ingredients:

4 Tablespoons of Tahini (sesame paste found near peanut butter)

3 cloves of garlic (roughly chopped)

1/3-1/2 cup of water

2 cans of garbanzo beans, drained and rinsed (or preferably use 1 can of soy beans for one of the garganzo's)

Juice from 2 lemons

5 shakes of Tabasco (or to taste)

1/2 teaspoon salt

Directions:

1. First, you empty beans into a food processor.
2. After which you add garlic, Tahini, lemon juice, Tabasco, salt and ½ cup water.
3. After that, you process for a few minutes to blend.
4. Then you check for consistency and for a thinner dip, add more water.
5. Make sure you serve with crackers, Veggie or apple slices.

Edam me Dip

makes about 2 cups
Ingredients:

½ cup of tightly packed fresh cilantro

¼ cup of freshly squeezed lime (or better still lemon) juice

1 small avocado

Salt to taste (be very careful because the miso is salty)

About 10 oz. package of shelled edamame, cooked per directions on the bag and rinsed with cold water

1 large clove garlic (roughly chopped)

½ of a 6 oz. container plain yogurt

1 ½ Tablespoons of miso (Japanese paste-like flavoring made from fermented soybeans)

5 shakes of Tabasco

Remember that you can leave out the miso, but you'll need to pump up the other flavors - Tabasco, lime, garlic)

Directions:

1. First, you place drained edamame in a food processor and pulse several times.
2. After which you add the chopped cilantro and pulse again.
3. After that, you add the remaining ingredients and pulse until well pureed.
4. At this point, you add more water if it needs to be thinned slightly.
5. Finally, you serve with sliced vegetables or whole grain crackers.

Roasted Carrot and Garlic Hummus

Serves 6-8
Ingredients:

3 cloves garlic (unpeeled)

1 15 oz. of can of garbanzo beans (rinsed and drained)

7-8 shakes of Tabasco Sauce

½ teaspoon of ground Coriander

Scant amount of water

3/4 lb. of carrots, peeled and roughly chopped

1 raw clove garlic (roughly chopped)

2 Tablespoons of Tahini

Juice from 2 Lemons (it all depends on tartness)

About ½ teaspoon of salt

Directions:

1. Meanwhile, you heat oven to 425 degrees.
2. After which you place the carrots and the unpeeled garlic on a baking sheet and into the preheated oven.
3. After that, you roast for about 20 minutes or until the carrots are tender (NOTE: Be careful not to overcook the garlic as it will start to brown in areas).
4. At this point, you cool slightly
5. Furthermore, you peel the roasted garlic and place into the bowl of a food processor along with the carrots and the 1 raw garlic clove.
6. After which you add the drained garbanzo beans, hummus, lemon juice, Tabasco, Coriander and salt.

7. Then you process on high, stopping to scrape down the sides of the bowl until blended.
8. This is when you add a bit of water and continue to process until the desired consistency (about 1/8 cup or less).
9. Finally, you serve with crackers or your favorite sliced veggies.

Roasted Red Pepper Dip

**Serves 6-8
Ingredients**:

2 slices of bread (I prefer Udi's gluten-free bread)

1 Tablespoons of fresh lemon juice

2 large clove garlic (roughly chopped)

½ teaspoon of salt or to taste

1 cup of jarred roasted red peppers (rinsed and drained)

½ cup of chopped walnuts

½ teaspoon of ground cumin

¼ teaspoon of red pepper flakes

Directions:

1. First, you combine all ingredients in a food processor.
2. After which you pulse until smooth.
3. Finally, you transfer to a serving bowl and serve with pita, crackers or sliced raw vegetables like carrots, jicama, and celery.

PLANT BASE SOUP AND SALAD RECIPES

Creamy Curried Cauliflower Soup

Serves 5-6

Ingredients:

½ lb. of yams peeled and cut into 1 1/2" pieces

1 ½ cups of sliced carrots (3 medium)

½ cup of chopped onion

3 teaspoons of curry powder

½ teaspoon of salt

1 (14-oz) can unsweetened light coconut milk

½ lb. of potatoes (peeled and cut into 1 1/2" pieces)

One large head of cauliflower cut into about 1 1/2" pieces

¾ cup of coarsely chopped red pepper (1 medium)

1 (15-oz) can garbanzo beans (rinsed and drained)

2 teaspoons of grated fresh ginger

1/8 teaspoon of crushed red pepper

4 cups of vegetable broth

Directions:

1. First, you combine potatoes, cauliflower, carrots, sweet pepper, onion, and beans in a large pot.

2. After which you sprinkle curry powder, ginger and red pepper and salt over vegetables and beans.
3. After that, you pour broth over all.
4. At this point, you bring to a boil, cover and cook on low-heat for about 1 hour or until vegetables are tender.
5. Finally, you stir in coconut milk and heat through.

Note: If you are using a slow cooker, set on high for 4 hours or low for 8.

Curried Coconut Lentil Yam Soup

Serves 6

Ingredients:

1 can of garbanzo beans (drained and rinsed)

1 (14 oz.) can crushed tomatoes

1 ½ teaspoons of curry powder

1 teaspoon of cumin

3 garlic cloves (minced)

1 ½ tablespoons of maple syrup or better still sugar replacement

2 Tablespoons of peanut butter

1 (3-4 cups) large sweet potato, peeled and cubed

½ cup of red lentils (rinsed)

4 cups of low-sodium vegetable broth

½ -1 teaspoon of garam masala

1 Tablespoon of minced ginger

¼ teaspoon of cinnamon

2 cups of soy milk (or substitute) mixed with 1 ½ teaspoons of coconut extract

Directions:

1. First, you combine all the ingredients in a big soup pot.
2. After which you heat to boiling and then lower it to a simmer and cook covered for about 45 minutes to an hour.
3. Enjoy!

Moroccan Stew with Kale

Ingredients:

Serves 6

2 teaspoons of ground cumin

1/2 teaspoon of ground cloves

½ teaspoon of ground turmeric

1 teaspoon of salt

2 cups of rough chopped kale

1 (about 14.5 oz.) can diced tomatoes (undrained)

4 large carrots (chopped)

3 large potatoes (I prefer Yukon gold's) peeled and chopped

1/2 cup of dried apricots (chopped)

1 tablespoon of cornstarch (it is optional)   1 tablespoon of water (optional)

2 teaspoons of ground cinnamon

1 teaspoon of ground ginger

½ teaspoon of ground nutmeg

½ teaspoon of curry powder

1 sweet onion (chopped)

1-quart vegetable stock (or better still more if you want it to be more soup-like)

1 tablespoon of honey

2 sweet potatoes (peeled and chopped)

1 (about 15 oz.) can garbanzo beans (drained)

1 cup dried lentils (rinsed)

Salt and Pepper to taste

Directions:

1. First, you cook onion on medium high heat in a little water or broth until soft and just beginning to brown, 5 to 10 minutes.
2. After which you stir in the spices and cook until they are fragrant.
3. After that, you pour the vegetable broth into the pot.
4. Then you add more if you want it to be more soup-like.
5. At this point, you stir in the tomatoes, honey, carrots, sweet potatoes, potatoes, garbanzo beans, apricots, and lentils.
6. This is when you bring to a boil and reduce heat to low.
7. Furthermore, you stir in the shredded kale.
8. After that, you simmer stew for 30 minutes until the vegetables and lentils are cooked and tender.
9. Finally, you season with salt and black pepper (NOTE: If desired, combine cornstarch and water and stir into stew).
10. Then you simmer until stew has thickened, about 5 minutes.

Hearty Vegetable Soup

Serves 6
Ingredients:

4-6 cups of water

2 medium bell peppers (coarsely chopped)

1 large onion (chopped)

1 bunch kale (washed, leaves removed from stems and chopped)

1 can red or better still pinto beans (drained and rinsed)

½ cup of red lentils

½ head cauliflower florets (bite-sized)

1 cup of carrots (cut 1/2 inch thick)

3 cloves garlic (chopped)

1 (14-oz.) can diced tomatoes

1 can pumpkin pie mix (or better still straight pumpkin)

Directions:

1. First, you place lentils and water in a large soup pot and begin to simmer.
2. After which you add all of the prepared vegetables to the pot and simmered covered for 30 minutes or until the vegetables are tender.
3. After that, you add more water if necessary.
4. Then you add the pumpkin and the beans and heat through.
5. Finally, you serve with a green salad.

Mushroom Quinoa Soup

Serves 4

Ingredients:

½ yellow onion (chopped)

8 oz. of mushrooms sliced (remember if they are large, cut them in half first)

½ cup of uncooked quinoa

1 teaspoon of oregano

2 Tablespoons of flour

Pepper to taste

¼ cup of water

2 cloves garlic (minced)

1 small zucchini, (cut in half lengthwise and sliced)

4 cups of veggie stock

½ teaspoon of thyme

1 cup of non-dairy milk

½ teaspoon of salt

Directions:

1. First, you sauté onions in water until translucent.

2. After which you add garlic and mushrooms and continue to sauté until mushrooms have started to wilt.

3. After that, you add zucchini, quinoa and stock and continue to cook until mushroom are done.

4. Then you mix ½ cup milk alternative with 2 Tablespoons of flour until smooth and add to mushroom mixture along with the other ½ cup of milk alternative.

5. Finally, you add salt and pepper to taste

Vegetable Soup with Ravioli

Serves 4

Ingredients:

1 cup of onion, chopped (or better still use 2 cups frozen bell pepper and onion mix, thawed and diced)

2 cloves garlic (minced)

One 28-ounce can crushed tomatoes (preferably fire-roasted)

1 teaspoon of dried basil or better still marjoram

About 5-6 stems kales (depending on size) rough chopped

Salt and freshly ground pepper to taste

1 cup bell peppers (chopped)

1 cup of carrots (peeled and chopped)

¼ teaspoon of crushed red pepper, or to taste (it is optional)

One 15-ounce can vegetable broth

1 cup of cannellini beans

One 6- to 9-ounce package fresh or better still frozen ravioli

2 cups of diced zucchini, (about 2 medium)

Directions:

1. First, you add about 2 Tablespoons of water to the soup pot and add peppers and onions, carrots and cook, stirring, for a few minutes.

2. After which you add the garlic and crushed red pepper and cook an addition minute.

3. After that, you add tomatoes, broth, water and basil (or marjoram), beans and kale; bring to a boil over high heat.

4. At this point, you season with salt and pepper to taste.

5. Then in a separate pan, boil enough water for the ravioli's and cooking according to package directions.

6. Finally, you add the cooked ravioli to each soup bowl and fill with soup.

Note: feel free to add the raviolis to the boiling soup pot itself, but be careful not to overcook. Remember, if they are prepared separately, they are less likely to fall apart, especially as leftovers.

Avocado, Papaya Gazpacho

Ingredients:

1 ½ cups of unsweetened pineapple juice

1 green (or better still any color bell pepper, seeded and diced)

1 avocado (cut into 1/4" dice)

6-10 dashed of Tabasco

Salt and ground pepper to taste

1 ½ cups of tomato juice or better still tomato-veggie juice

1 ripe papaya or better still mango, peeled, seeded and diced

½ red onion (diced)

¼ cup of fresh lime juice

¼ cup of finely chopped cilantro

Directions:

1. First, in a large bowl, gently mix all of the ingredients.
2. Then you cover and refrigerate for a couple of hours.

Tomato, Carrot, Brussels Sprout Soup

Serves 6

Ingredients:

1 medium onion (chopped)

2 carrots (peeled and cut into rounds)

3 cups of Brussels sprouts (cut in half or fourths)

½ cup of red lentils

One 8 oz. can tomato sauce

1/3 teaspoon of cinnamon

Salt and pepper to taste

4 cups of water

5 cloves garlic (minced)

1 large beet (peeled and cut into 1/2" cubes)

1/3 cup of green lentils

½ cup of canned kidney beans

2 cups of carrot juice

½ teaspoon of garam masala

2 Tablespoons of almond or peanut butter

Directions:

1. First, you bring 4 cups water to boil and add the green and red lentils.

2. After which you cook for a few minutes until they start to soften.

3. After that, you add the remainder of the vegetables, juice, tomato sauce, beans, spices and nut butter.

4. Then you simmer soup, covered for 30-45 minutes until the vegetables are crisp tender and the lentils are soft.

Lentil Pea Soup

Serves 6

Ingredients:

1 large onion (chopped)

1 cup of carrot (chopped)

2 teaspoons of ground coriander

1 ½ teaspoons of ground turmeric

1 ½ cup orange lentils

1 ½ cup of split peas

¼ cup of freshly squeezed lemon juice

Salt and pepper to taste

¼ cup of water

½ cup of celery (chopped)

6 cloves garlic (finely chopped)

2 teaspoons of ground cumin

¼ cup of all-purpose flour

1 ½ cup of green lentils

8 cups of vegetable broth

1 cup of low fat unsweetened canned coconut milk

Directions:

1. First, you heat water in a large pot and add the onion.

2.   After which you sauté a few minutes and then add the celery and carrot.

3.   After that, you add garlic and spices.

4.   Then you stir in the flour and cook for 1 minute.

5.   At this point, you pour in the broth and bring to a boil while whisking constantly.

6.   Furthermore, you add the lentils and peas to the thickened broth, lower the heat, and simmer, covered, until tender, about 45 minutes.

7.   Finally, you whisk in coconut milk (if using), lemon juice and season with salt and pepper.

Roasted Tomato Bisque

Serves 4

Ingredients:

1 red bell pepper (seeded and quartered)

4 garlic cloves (peeled)

½ - 1 cup of milk alternative like soy (**NOTE:** make sure it has nothing but beans and water)

Salt and pepper to taste

5 large tomatoes (quartered)

2 large yellow onions (quartered)

2 ½ cups of vegetable stock or water

½ teaspoon of paprika

Directions:

1. Meanwhile, you heat oven to 400 degrees F.
2. After which you line a large baking sheet with parchment paper and spread the tomatoes, onions and pepper onto it.
3. After that, you sprinkle with salt, pepper and paprika.
4. Then you bake in the oven for about 5 minutes and then add the garlic cloves.
5. At this point you continue to roast the vegetables until they soften and start to caramelize, about 25-25 minutes, stirring about halfway through.
6. Furthermore, you put the vegetables into a large soup pot and add the vegetable stock.

7. Make sure you use an immersion blender (or transfer to a blender) to process until smooth, in batches if necessary.
8. After that, you add ½ cup of the milk alternative and stir to combine.
9. Finally, you taste and add up to ½ cup more, if needed.
10. Then you season with salt, pepper, and more paprika.

Thai Carrot Soup

Serves 4

Ingredients:

1 Tablespoons of peeled, grated fresh ginger

2 cloves garlic (peeled and chopped)

3 cups of low-sodium vegetable stock (plus more as needed)

1-2 freshly squeezed limes (or better still lemons in a pinch)

¾ teaspoon of sea salt

1 medium yellow onion (chopped)

1 Tablespoon of Thai red curry paste (add more to taste - can be found in the Asian section of the store)

1 lb. of carrots, sliced (about 4 large)

1 (about 13.5-ounce) can light coconut milk

About 1/3 cup of fresh thymes leaves (minced).

Directions:

1. First, water sauté the onion until it is soft.
2. After which you stir in the ginger, curry paste, and garlic and cook while stirring until well combined and fragrant, about 1 minute.
3. After that you add the carrots, stock, lime juice and bring to a boil over high heat.
4. Then you reduce heat to low and simmer, covered, until the carrots are very tender, about 30 minutes.
5. At this point, you puree the soup in batches in a blender, using the hot fill line as a guide to reduce splatter.

6. Furthermore, you transfer the pureed soup back to the saucepan and place over low heat.
7. This is when you stir in the coconut milk and salt to taste.
8. After that, you simmer uncovered until the soup is heated through, about 20 minutes.
9. **Note:** If the soup is not spicy enough, I suggest you add more of the red curry paste.
10. Finally, you serve with a sprinkling of thyme leaves.

Roasted Cauliflower Soup

Serves 3-4

Ingredients:

1 onion (slice into thick moon)

1 teaspoon of curry powder

1 teaspoon of Thai red curry paste (it is optional)

¼ cup of ground cashews

1 head of cauliflower (cut into chunks)

2 lemons (juiced)

1 can of low-fat coconut milk

2 cups of water or better still vegetable juice (pour over ice to chill if you are serving chilled)

1 teaspoon of salt

Directions:

1. Meanwhile, you heat oven to 400 degrees.
2. After which you lightly spray a baking sheet with oil. Spread cauliflower and onion over sheet.
3. After that, you drizzle lemon, curry powder and ½ teaspoon of salt over vegetables.
4. Then you mix with your hand to combine.
5. At this point, you bake in oven for about 20-15 minutes or until mostly tender.
6. Furthermore, you Let cool for a few minutes on the counter.
7. After that, you add the coconut milk, lemon, red curry paste and remaining salt to the container of your high-speed blender and slowly increase speed until the soup is blended to smoothness.

8. This is when you add more water or stock as needed to thin and adjust seasonings to your taste, adding more heat from the Thai curry paste or more salt.
9. In addition, you chill in refrigerator or if you really in a hurry, in the freezer for about 10 minutes.
10. Remember, if you want to serve it hot, I suggest you pour soup into a pan and heat through.
11. Finally, you top with a few teaspoons of ground cashews for decoration and crunch.

Cold Cucumber Soup

Serves 6

Ingredients:

¼ of a red onion (roughly chopped)

8 large mint leaves

2 Tablespoons of lemon juice

½ - ¾ cup of water

Salt to taste

1 ¾ lbs. of cucumbers (peeled, seeded and cut into 3" pieces)

1 garlic clove (skinned)

1 teaspoon of maple syrup

6 oz. plain homemade or better still store-bought soy yogurt

Avocado (chopped)

Directions:

1. First, you place all the ingredients in a Vitamix or food processor with ½ cup of the spring water.

2. After which you pulse a few times so the ingredients are coarsely chopped, then process until smooth.

3. After that, you thin with more water if needed.

4. Then you transfer to a bowl and refrigerate for 2 hours or overnight, until well chilled.

5. Finally, you ladle soup into soup bowls and top with the chopped avocado.

Tomato Coconut Curry Soup
Serve 6-8
Ingredients:
1 cup of finely chopped onion

1 carrot (peeled and finely chopped)

16 ounces can (diced or better still stewed tomatoes)

½ teaspoon of curry powder

½ cup of light coconut milk

Salt and pepper to taste

Chopped parsley (for garnish)

¼ cup of water

1 stalk celery (finely chopped)

2 yams (peeled and diced)

1 to 2 cups of water or stock

¼ teaspoon of ground coriander

1/3 cup of nutritional yeast (optional)

a couple pinches of hot pepper flakes

Directions:
1. First, you heat water in a large pot over medium heat.

2. After which you add the onion and celery.

3. After that, you sauté for about 10 to 15 minutes, until the celery has softened.

4. Then you add the spices and stir to combine.

5. At this point, you add the carrot and potatoes and sauté for 10 more minutes.

6. Furthermore, you add the tomatoes and 1 to 2 cups of water or broth and bring to a boil.

7. After that, you lower the heat, cover and cook for about 30 to 35 minutes, until the potatoes are tender.

8. This is when you set aside to cool for a few minutes.

9. In addition, you blend in small batches so the hot soup won't splatter.

10. After which you return the puree to the pot, add the coconut milk and continue cooking for 5 minutes.

11. Finally, you taste and adjust the seasonings.

12. Then garnish with chopped parsley

Curried Chickpea Rice Salad

Serve 6

Ingredients:

Dressing:

4 teaspoons of lime juice

½ teaspoon of salt

4 teaspoons of apple cider vinegar

4 teaspoons of curry powder

4 teaspoons of maple syrup

Salad:

2 teaspoons of whole cumin seeds (toasted briefly in a dry pan, until fragrant).

1 red bell pepper (cored, seeded and chopped)

2 cups of cooked brown rice

½ cup of seedless raisins

1 cans of cooked chickpeas (rinsed and drained)

2/3 cup of finely chopped red onion

1 cup of cilantro or parsley (chopped)

One package firm tofu, drained, pressed for about 20 minutes, cut into cubes. Make sure you marinated with your favorite marinade for at least 5 minutes. Then you bake in a 400-degree oven for 10-15 minutes, turn and bake another 15 minutes

Directions:

1. First, in a small bowl, whisk together vinegar, lime juice, curry powder, maple syrup and salt.

2. After which in a large bowl add raisins, cumin, chickpeas, bell pepper, onion and cilantro and toss to combine.

3. Finally, you pour on dressing, & mix well.

Roasted Cauliflower and Mushroom Salad

Serves 2

Ingredients:

Salt and pepper to taste

½ head cauliflower, broken into bite-sized pieces

8 oz. of mushrooms (halved scant olive oil)

Ingredients for the Dressing:

1 teaspoons of mustard

1 teaspoon of maple syrup

1/3 cup of balsamic vinegar

1 clove garlic (minced)

Directions:

1. First, you toss the cauliflower and mushrooms on a baking sheet with a scant amount of olive oil (or try it without any).

2. After which you add salt and pepper.

3. After that, you roast in a preheated 400-degree F oven until they start to caramelize, about 20-30 minutes, flipping half way through.

4. Then you prepare dressing in a separate bowl and pour over vegetables.

5. Finally, you serve over lettuce of your choice or eat as is.

6. Enjoy.

Kale Salad with Oranges

Serves 6

Ingredients:

1 packaged kale salad mix or preferably from scratch:

　1 carrot (grated)

½ cup walnuts (chopped)

1 whole avocado (1/2 rough chopped, 1/2 for massaging into kale)

　1 bunch of kale (stems removed and chopped)

　1 cup of shredded red cabbage

1 can mandarin oranges (drained, reserving 2 Tablespoon juice)

Ingredients for the Dressing:

1 teaspoon of maple syrup

1/3 cup of apple cider vinegar

2 tablespoons of juice from the mandarin oranges

Directions:

1. First, you combine all salad ingredients in a large bowl.

2. After which you add ½ of the avocado and massage into kale with hands until it softens.

3. Then you prepare the dressing in a separate bow.

4. Finally, you pour over all and toss.

Roasted Potato & Green Bean Salad

Serves 4

Ingredients

1-2 yams (peeled and cut into chunks)

½ red onion (sliced thinly)

1 Tablespoon of grainy or better still regular mustard

3 medium sized potatoes (peeled and cut into chunks)

3 cups of green beans (trimmed and cut into 1 1/2" pieces)

1/3 cup of balsamic or better still red wine vinegar

Optional: Kalamata olives (or better still any olives you have on hand)

Salt and pepper to taste

Directions:

1. First, you steam the green beans for about 10 minutes until tender.

2. After which you roast the potatoes in a 400-degree oven 10 minutes until tender (**NOTE**: to keep from sticking to the pan, you can add a little non-stick spray).

3. After that, you mix the beans and potatoes with the red onion and optional olives.

4. Then you prepare the dressing and pour over vegetables.

5. Finally, you mix to combine, adding salt and pepper to taste.

Roasted Yam, Onion and Mushroom Salad

Serves 2

Ingredients

2 yams (peeled and cut into large chunks)

One 8 oz. box of mushrooms sliced

½ head of romaine lettuce (torn into bite-sized pieces)

1 onion (peeled and cut into large chunks)

Ingredients for the Dressing:

2 teaspoons of maple syrup

1/8 cup of balsamic vinegar

2 teaspoons of jarred mustard

Directions:

1. Meanwhile you heat oven to 375 degrees.

2. After which you place chopped yam and onions on a non-stick cookie sheet and into the preheated oven.

3. After that, you roast for about 20 minutes or until tender.

4. Then you sauté mushrooms in water or broth until tender.

5. At this point, you put lettuce, yams, onions and mushrooms into a large salad bowl.

6. Finally, you mix all of the dressing ingredients in a small bowl and pour over the salad ingredients, toss and serve.

Corn, Tomato, Avocado Salad

Serves 4

Ingredients:

1 box of grape tomatoes (halved)

¼ cup of chopped red onion

Salt and pepper to taste

2 ears of corn (with kernels cut off)

1 avocado (large chopped)

2 Tablespoons of basil minced

Juice of one lemon or better still lime

Directions:

1. First, you water sauté the corn in about ¼ cup water for 3-5 minutes.

2. Then when it is done, put into a plate and cool in the frig.

3. After that, you add tomatoes, corn, avocado, red onion and basil to a large mixing bowl.

4. At this point, you add the lemon or lime juice, salt and pepper and mixed carefully to combine.

5. Finally, you let sit for a few minutes for flavors to mix.

Directions on how to remove the kernels:

First, you stand corn on its end and run a knife down the sides until all the kernels are cut off.

Feel free to also stand it inside of a large bowl if you don't want a mess on your counter.

Quinoa Salad with Spicy Peanut Dressing

Serves 4

Ingredients:

2 cups of water

½ medium cucumber (seeds removed and chopped 1/4")

1 medium carrot (cut into julienne strips)

1 hand full of arugula (chopped)

3 Tablespoons of smooth peanut butter

3 Tablespoons of tamari or soy sauce

1 small clove garlic (minced)

1 cup of quinoa

½ red onion (chopped)

½ cup of black beans

1 stalk broccoli (chopped ¼)

¼ cup of cilantro, mint, or better still basil chopped

3 Tablespoons of rice vinegar

½ teaspoon of hot red pepper flakes

Directions:

1. First, you bring 2 cups of water to a boil in a medium saucepan.

2. After which you add quinoa and simmer briskly until quinoa is tender, about 15 minutes.

3. In the meantime, in a large bowl, combine peanut butter, vinegar, soy sauce, hot red pepper flakes, and garlic.

4. After that, you add enough hot tap water (about 2 tablespoons) to thin the mixture to sauce consistency.

5. Then when quinoa is ready, transfer it to the bowl, along with the veggies, arugula and cilantro, and toss to combine.

6. Finally, you refrigerated for 30 minutes to intensify the flavor.

PLANT BASED DESSERT RECIPES

Pumpkin Spice Chia Pudding

Serves 4-6

Ingredients:

1 cup of organic pumpkin puree

1 teaspoon of vanilla extract

½ cup of chia seeds (can be found in most health food stores).

2 cups of unsweetened organic almond milk

2 Tablespoons of almond butter

¼ cup of maple syrup or better still honey (see note below: to cut down on the sugar, I suggest you use 1 teaspoon of liquid Stevia)

2 teaspoons of pumpkin spice (or better still use 1 teaspoon of cinnamon, ¼ teaspoon of ginger, pinch ground clove, pinch allspice. (NOTE: recipe didn't call for it but you could also add 1/4 teaspoon of cardamom if you're adventurous.)

Some optional toppings: pumpkin seeds, chopped walnuts or pecans, shredded coconut or small chocolate chips.

Directions:

1. First, you pour 1 cup of almond milk into a glass bowl and add pumpkin puree.

2. After which you whisk until the puree is completely dissolved.

3. After that, you add the almond butter, vanilla, maple syrup and pumpkin spice and whisk till incorporated.

4. Then you add remaining almond milk and begin adding the chia seeds, whisking to mix.

5. Furthermore, you let stand for 5 minutes and then whisk to incorporate the chia seeds throughout the pudding.

6. After that, you place in the refrigerator for 15 minutes then remove and whisk again.

7. Finally, you chill in the fridge for about 30 minutes to allow the pudding to set.

8. **NOTE:** If you are using Stevia, I suggest you start with about 1/3 teaspoon and work up to the sweetness you like.

Baked Pears with Cardamom

Serves 2-4

Ingredients:

½ teaspoon of ground cardamom

2-4 firm ripe pears (halved and seeded)

2 Tablespoons of sugar

¼ cup of white wine

1 teaspoon of vanilla

1 ½ Tablespoons of lemon juice

Directions:

1. Meanwhile, you heat oven to 400 degrees F.

2. After which you combine wine, cardamom and vanilla in 8" square baking dish.

3. After that, you place pears cut-side up in baking dish and pour lemon juice over.

4. Then you sprinkle with sugar.

5. At this point, you cover pan with foil, place on the middle rack in the over, and bake 30 minutes, or until tender.

6. Furthermore, you remove foil and move pan to top rack.

7. After that, you broil for 5 minutes, or until lightly browned (**NOTE:** make sure you watch carefully).

8. Finally, you transfer pears to a serving plate and drizzle with juice from the pan.

Raspberry Jell-O

Serves 6

Ingredients:

1 ½ cups of water

½ cup of walnuts

1/8 cup of maple syrup or better still other sugar

2 packages of frozen raspberries (defrosted).

8 ounces (1 cup) vegan sour cream or better still plain soy yogurt (6 oz.)

3 Tablespoons of Agar-agar flakes (in the Asian section of the grocery store)

½ teaspoon of liquid stevia (orange flavored)

Directions:

1. First, you drain the liquid from the defrosted raspberries and put them in a large bowl.

2. After which you add the liquid to water to make 1 ½ cups.

3. After that, you heat water/raspberry juice in a small saucepan and add agar-agar.

4. Then you stir until dissolve then set aside to cool for a few minutes.

5. Meanwhile, you add the sour cream or soy yogurt to the bowl of raspberries along with the walnuts.

6. At this point when the agar-agar has dissolved you add it to the bowl of raspberries.

7. This is when you stir to combine completely.

8. Finally, you refrigerate in this bowl, a mold or small serving containers until it is set.

Green Berry Smoothie

Serves 1

Ingredients:

1 cup of your favorite non-dairy drink (I prefer hemp or almond milk)

Fiber and / or powdered greens (it is optional)

1 cups of frozen berries, any mix (organic strawberries, blueberries, cranberries are my favorite)

½ cup of water for thinning

1-2 leaves Swiss chard broken into smaller bits

Directions:

1. First, you add the berries, Swiss chard and on-dairy drink to the blender

2. After which you whir until smooth, adding water to thick to the consistency you like.

3. Then you add any fiber, powdered greens or protein powder you like and whir just a few more seconds.

Chocolate Chip Chickpea Cookies

Makes about 24 cookies

Ingredients:

½ cup of almond butter (or better still peanut butter)

1/3 cup of oat flour (you can still make this with old fashioned oats in a blender)

1 teaspoon of cinnamon

½ teaspoon of salt

½ cup of chopped walnuts

One (15 oz.) can of chickpeas (drained)

½ cup of honey or maple syrup (to cut the sugar in half, sub. ½ teaspoon of liquid Stevia for ¼ cup)

1 Tablespoon of vanilla

2 teaspoons of baking powder

½ cup of chocolate chips

Directions:

1. Meanwhile, you heat oven to 350 degrees and line a cookie sheet with parchment paper.

2. After which you add chickpeas, almond butter, honey, flour, vanilla, cinnamon, baking powder and salt to the bowl of a food processor.

3. After that, you process until mixture is completely smooth, scraping down the sides to incorporate all.

4. At this point, you remove to a bowl and stir in chocolate chips and walnuts.

5. Then you drop by teaspoons onto parchment paper and spread them out slightly with the back of your spoon.

6. Finally, you bake for 25 minutes or until the sides turn a bit brown.

Groovy Green Smoothie

Serves 1

Ingredients:

One orange peeled into sections

½ scoop of Super Seed

1 cup of frozen organic berries

3 romaine lettuce leaves

¾ cup of almond milk

Directions:

1. First, you put all into blender except the Super Seed.

2. After which you blend until smooth.

3. After that, you add a little water if too thick.

4. Then you pour in the Super Seed and whir just a few seconds.

Homemade Soy Yogurt

Serves 6-7

Ingredients:

1 box of regular or better still unsweetened soy milk (not chilled). I prefer West soy Unsweetened Vanilla.

Yogurt Starter like Yogourmet (available in the yogurt section of Whole Foods Market.)

3 Tablespoons of cornstarch

1-2 Tablespoons of sugar or better still maple syrup

Candy thermometer

Directions:

1. First, you add 2 cups of soy milk to a saucepan and start heating.

2. After which you pour ½ cup of cold soy milk into a measuring cup and whisk in 3 Tablespoons of cornstarch.

3. Then once the milk in the saucepan starts to steam, you whisk in the cornstarch mixture.

4. At this point, you continue to heat and whisk until it starts to thicken.

5. Furthermore, you remove from the heat.

6. After whisk in the rest of the soy milk and let the temperature come down to at least 110 degrees F.

7. Finally, you whisk in the starter to blend and pour into the containers.

8. Remember to follow the instruction on your yogurt maker for time.

Strawberry Ice Cream

Serves 4-6

Ingredients:

One bag of frozen organic strawberries

One cup of almond milk (or better still any milk alternative you like)

3 bananas (peeled, rough chopped, put into baggies and frozen)

2/3 cup of raw cashews (soaked for several hours)

4 pitted medjool dates (it is optional)

Directions:

1. First, you put frozen bananas, strawberries, drained and soaked cashews, dates, and almond milk into the jar of a high-powered blender.

2. After which you blend, turning off frequently to scrape down the sides and help the blender to work.

3. After that, you add more milk if it seems too thick.

4. Then you serve immediately or pour into a freezer safe dish and freeze.

NOTE: you will need to let it defrost a little to get the ice cream back to creaminess.

5. Finally, you top with walnuts or pistachios and sliced strawberries, if you like.

Black Bean Brownies

Serves 6

Ingredients:

2 whole, ripe bananas

¼ cup of sugar

½ tablespoon of cinnamon

½ cup of regular or better still non-dairy chocolate chips

½ cup of instant oats or oat flour (preferably made in a food processor from raw oats)

15 ounces no-salt black beans (drained and rinsed)

¼ cup of maple syrup

¼ cup of unsweetened cacao (I like the KIVA brand).

1 teaspoon of vanilla extract

½ cup of chopped walnuts (it is optional)

Directions:

1. Meanwhile, you heat oven to 350 degrees F.

2. After which you lightly coat an 8×6″ pan with cooking spray.

3. After that, you combine all ingredients, except oats, in a food processor.

4. Then you blend until smooth.

5. At this point, you stir in the oat flour / oats until blended well.

6. Furthermore, you fold in chocolate chips and nuts.

7. After that, you pour batter into the pan.

8. Finally, you bake for 30-35 minutes or until a toothpick comes out clean.

Blueberry Lemon Coconut Bars

Serves 6-8

Ingredients:

3 Tablespoons of chia seeds

½ cup of old fashioned oats

1 cup of shredded coconut

½ teaspoon of salt

1 cup of frozen or better still fresh blueberries

1/3 cup of honey or better still maple syrup

6 Tablespoons of fresh lemon juice

1 ½ cups of old fashioned oats, ground into flour in a blender

2 Tablespoons of lemon zest

1 teaspoon of baking powder

½ cup of walnuts (chopped)

2/3 cup of apple sauce

¼ cup of coconut oil (melted)

Directions:

1. First, you heat the oven to 350 degrees and line an 8 x 8" baking dish with parchment paper.

2. After which in a small bowl, mix the chia seeds with the lemon juice and set aside to thicken.

3. After that, you mix the dry ingredients, oat flour, oats, coconut, baking powder, salt, with the walnuts and blueberries in a large bowl.

4. At this point, you mix the wet ingredients, the apple sauce, coconut oil, honey or maple syrup and soaked chia seeds in another bowl.

5. Then you pour the dry ingredients into the wet and stir until combined.

NOTE: feel free to use your hands to make sure all is combined.

6. Remember the dough will be pretty dry.

7. Furthermore, you press the dough into your prepared pan, leveling the top with your spoon.

8. This is when you bake in your preheated oven for about 30 minutes or until the edges begin to brown.

9. Finally, you let cool before removing from the pan.

10. Make sure you cut into squares.

Carrot Pudding with Indian Spices

Serves 4-6

Ingredients:

1 ½ cups of unsweetened almond milk (split)

½ chia seeds (NOTE: light is best for color, but any will do)

1 teaspoon of vanilla extract

¼ teaspoon of ground ginger

¼ teaspoon of ground cloves

5-6 peeled and shredded carrots (NOTE: I shred mine in the food processor)

1 cup of light coconut milk (split)

¼ cup of maple syrup or better still honey (to reduce the sugar, I suggest you add 1/8 cup honey or syrup plus 1/3 teaspoon of liquid stevia)

1/3 teaspoon of ground cardamom (however, this is a pretty strong spice to use sparingly, taste and add more if needed)

½ teaspoon of ground cinnamon

Directions:

1. First, you place the shredded carrots and ½ cup almond plus ½ cup coconut milk in a saucepan over medium heat.

2. After which you add the spices and cook until the carrots are tender, about 20 minutes.

3. After that, you set aside to cool for a few minutes.

4. Then when the carrots are slightly cooled, add them and the cooking liquid to a blender.

5. Blend until smooth, adding some of the almond milk to thin if it gets too thick.

6. At this point, you add the remainder of the milks and the sweetener and blend slower to combine.

7. Furthermore, you pour into a large bowl and add the chia seeds, mixing well.

8. After that, you put the bowl into the refrigerator to cool, stirring after about 15 minutes to make sure the chia seeds stay suspended.

9. This time you continue to cool until set.

10. Finally, you serve in individual bowls and top with chopped walnuts, pumpkin seeds or mini chocolate chips.

PLANT BASED MAIN DISH RECIPES
Sweet and Sour Tofu

Serves 4

Ingredients:

ingredients for the Tofu:

1/3 cup of soy sauce

3 Tablespoons of ketchup

One dash hot sauce

¼ teaspoon of ground black pepper

One (16 oz.) container firm tofu, drained, halved crosswise and pressed for 20 minutes.

2 Tablespoons of maple syrup

2 Tablespoons of rice vinegar

¼ teaspoon of garlic powder

Ingredient for Stir-Fry:

1 large bell peppers (cut into chunks)

2 large carrots (sliced)

2 cups of cooked quinoa or rice

1 large red onion (cut into chunks)

2 cloves garlic (crushed)

2 cups of pineapple chunks

Directions:

1. Meanwhile, you heat oven to 375 degrees.

Direction on how to prepare the tofu by pressing:

2. First, you cut tofu in half lengthwise and put between newspapers after first covering with paper towel.

3. After which you place a large container weighted down with canned food on top.

4. After that, you stress for at least 30 minutes.

5. At this point, you then cut tofu into inch sized pieces.

6. This is when you prepare marinade in a wide container and place pressed tofu into it for another 30 minutes, covering on all sides.

7. Furthermore, you lightly coat a non-stick cookie sheet with spray and place marinade tofu cubes on sheets keeping them separated.

8. Remember to reserve some marinade for the sauce.

9. Then you bake for about 15 minutes, flip tofu and cook for another 15 minutes until toasty brown.

10. Meanwhile, you place onion, carrot, peppers, and garlic in a large fry pan with about ½ cup water.

11. After that, you lightly boil until veggies are crisp-tender.

12. At this point you add the pineapple chunks along with the reserved marinade and stir to coat vegetables.

13. Finally, you cook through to heat and serve over quinoa or rice.

Broccoli Cauliflower Veggie Divan

Serves 6

Ingredients:

½ head cauliflower (chopped into large pieces)

1 large yellow onion (chopped)

1 cup of milk alternative

2 Tablespoons of fresh lemon juice

¼ teaspoon of nutmeg

pinch of cayenne pepper

1 head of broccoli (chopped into large pieces)

4 large carrots (chopped)

2 cups of veggie broth

3 Tablespoons of flour (I prefer oatmeal made into flour in my vitamixer)

½ teaspoons of curry (it is optional)

Salt and pepper to taste

Directions:

1. Meanwhile, you heat oven to 350 degrees.

2. After which you sauté onion with a little water in a large sauté pan until almost soft.

3. After that, you mix flour with a little stock in a small bowl using a whisk.

4. At this point, you put the vegetables into a steamer and steam until crisp tender.

5. Then you add the veggie stock to the onions in the pan and heat a few minutes.

6. Furthermore, you add the flour / stock mixture to the pan and stir until well blended.

7. At this point, no lumps should form and mixture should begin to thicken.

8. After which you add the milk alternative to thin along with the lemon and spices.

9. Then when veggies are done, you put them into a casserole dish sprayed with a little non-stick spray.

10. In addition, you pour thickened sauce over veggies and move them around a bit so the sauce can sink down toward the bottom.

11. After that, you cover with foil and bake in the preheated oven for about 30 minutes until veggies are heated through.

12. Finally, you serve over your choice of grain

Moroccan Stew with Kale

Ingredients:

Serves 6

2 teaspoons of ground cumin

½ teaspoon of ground cloves

½ teaspoon of ground turmeric

1 teaspoon of salt

2 cups of rough chopped kale

1 (about 14.5 oz.) can diced tomatoes (undrained)

4 large carrots (chopped)

3 large potatoes (I prefer Yukon gold's) peeled and chopped

1/2 cup of dried apricots (chopped)

1 tablespoon of cornstarch (it is optional)

1 tablespoon of water (it is optional)

2 teaspoons of ground cinnamon

1 teaspoon of ground ginger

½ teaspoon of ground nutmeg

½ teaspoon of curry powder

1 sweet onion (chopped)

1-quart vegetable stock (or better still more if you want it to be more soup-like)

1 tablespoon of honey

2 sweet potatoes (peeled and chopped)

1 (about 15 oz.) can garbanzo beans, drained

1 cup of dried lentils (rinsed)

Salt and Pepper to taste

Directions:

1. First, you cook onion on medium high heat in a little water or broth until soft and just beginning to brown, 5 to 10 minutes.

2. After which you stir in the spices and cook until they are fragrant.

3. After that, you pour the vegetable broth into the pot.

4. At this point, you add more if you want it to be more soup-like.

5. Then you stir in the tomatoes, honey, carrots, sweet potatoes, potatoes, garbanzo beans, apricots, and lentils.

6. This is when you bring to a boil and reduce heat to low.

7. Furthermore, you stir in the shredded kale.

8. After that, you simmer stew for 30 minutes until the vegetables and lentils are cooked and tender.

9. Then you season with salt and black pepper.

10. However, if desired, combine cornstarch and water and stir into stew.

11. Finally, you simmer until stew has thickened, about 5 minutes.

Thai Curried Potatoes with Chard

Serves 6

Ingredients:

4 large potatoes (peeled and cut into 1" pieces)

2 bunches of Swiss chard (stems removed and rough chopped)

½ -3/4 can light coconut milk

1 large onion (sliced)

One (26 oz.) can diced tomatoes

2 teaspoons of red curry paste (or better still 2 teaspoons curry powder)

Salt and pepper to taste

Directions:

1. First, you sauté onion in a small amount of water for a few minutes.

2. After which you add all of the potatoes and the diced tomatoes, the red curry paste and about ¼ cup water so the potatoes don't stick.

3. After which you cover and continue to cook for around 5 minutes until potatoes start to soften.

4. After that, you add the chopped Swiss chard and continue to cook until chard wilts and softens, using a spatula to flip the potatoes over the chard.

5. Then you add the coconut milk and cook until potatoes and done and the sauce has reduced a bit.

Pasta with Spinach Marinara Sauce

Ingredients:

Serves 4

½ chopped onion (red or yellow)

½ cup of sun-dried tomatoes (sliced)

½ large package of frozen spinach or better still 10 oz. box

½ package tempeh (cubed)

1/3 teaspoon of garam masala

spaghetti pasta

¼ cup of water

3 large cloves garlic (sliced)

1/3 cup of seedless olives (sliced)

1 jar of your favorite marinara sauce

½ teaspoon of curry

Crumbled goat cheese (it is optional)

salt and pepper to taste

Directions:

1. First, you sauté onion in water until translucent.

2. After which you add sun-dried tomatoes, olives and frozen spinach, tempeh and marinara sauce.

3. After that, you add spices and sliced garlic and stir to combine.

4. At this point, you cook pasta according to the package directions.

5. Finally, you arrange past on the plate and scoop pasta with spinach over

Falafel Burger

Makes 3-4 patties

Ingredients:

2 garlic cloves (smashed)

¼ cup of parsley (chopped)

½ teaspoon of cumin

¼ teaspoon of cayenne

¾ teaspoon of salt

3 dashes of Tabasco sauce

Sliced tomatoes, red onion, lettuce and tahini dressing for serving

One 15 oz. can of garbanzo beans (chickpeas)

1 small onion (chopped)

¼ cup of mint (chopped)

½ teaspoon of coriander

1/3 teaspoon of baking soda

Juice of 1 lemon

Chickpea flour

Burger buns or better still pita bread

Ingredients for the Tahini Dressing:

Juice of 1 lemon

Salt to taste

¼ cup of tahini

Directions:

1. Meanwhile, you heat oven to 400 degrees.

2. After which you place half of garbanzo beans in a food processor a pulse a few times until chopped, but not smooth.

3. After that, you transfer to a large bowl.

4. Then you place remaining garbanzos in food processor with herbs, garlic, onion, spices, baking soda, salt, and lemon juice.

5. At this point, you pulse to a thick paste.

6. Furthermore, you transfer to bowl with chopped garbanzos.

7. After that, you add enough chickpea flour to make them easy to handle.

8. This is when you stir to combine.

9. Then you shape into patties and place onto a sprayed baking sheet.

10. Bake for about 15 to 20 minutes, flipping burgers half way through until golden and firm.

11. Finally, you serve with all of the fixins' and a dollop of tahini dressing.

Vegetarian Chili

Serves 4

Ingredients:

1 yellow onion (chopped)

2 medium large carrots (peeled and chopped)

1 bell pepper (chopped)

1 large can of pinto beans (or better still a mixture of any you like)

1/3 cup of quinoa (rinsed)

1-2 Tablespoons of chili powder

¼ teaspoon of cinnamon

½ teaspoon of dried oregano

Salt and pepper to taste

¼ cup of water

2 cloves garlic (minced)

2-3 stalks of celery (chopped)

1 medium-large zucchini (large chopped)

One (28 oz.) can of diced tomatoes

1-2 cups of tempeh (chopped)

½ teaspoon of cumin

¼ teaspoon of garam masala

1 avocado (sliced)

3 oz. of plain yogurt (it is optional)

Directions:

1. First, you add the water to the pan and sauté the onion about 5 minutes.

2. After which you add the garlic and all of the other vegetables except the zucchini.

3. After that, you sauté about 10 minutes.

4. Then you add the spices and salt and pepper to taste.

5. At this point, you add the canned tomatoes, beans, quinoa and tempeh, along with 1 cup water, stirring to combine.

6. This is when you cook another 10 minutes and add more water if it becomes too thick.

7. In addition, you add the zucchini and cook until zucchini is soften but not mushy.

8. Finally, you serve with sliced avocado.

Asian Noodle Salad

Serves 4-6

Ingredients:

4 scallions (chopped)

3 cups of snow peas (with string removed and cut into thirds)

One (12 ounce) of package of pasta

2 carrots (grated)

1 small red pepper (cut into small strips)

1/3 cup of fresh cilantro (chopped)

Dressing:

1/3 cup of reduced sodium soy sauce

2 Tablespoons of chili garlic sauce

1 Tablespoon of minced ginger

¼ cup of peanut butter

2 Tablespoons of rice vinegar

1 Tablespoon of sugar

Directions:

1. First, you boil pasta in a large pot of water until tender (al dente).

2. After which you drain, reserving a little pasta water.

3. After that while pasta is cooking, with a whisk, blend the peanut butter, soy sauce, vinegar, chili garlic sauce, sugar, and ginger until smooth.

4. Then you add a little pasta water if it's too thick.

5. This is when you cook the snow peas in scant water for about 3-5 minutes.

6. Furthermore, you add them to a large bowl with the other vegetables.

7. After which you add cooked pasta and pour dressing over.

8. Finally, you toss well to coat.

Lightly Curried Vegetable Wraps

Serves 8

Ingredients:

½ red bell pepper (diced)

4 cloves garlic (minced)

4 Cups of chopped vegetables, such as broccoli, carrots, steamed potatoes, zucchini, cauliflower, green beans, or use any you have on hand.

½ cup of hummus (or 8 teaspoons of crumbled feta cheese - optional.)

½ green bell pepper (diced)

1 medium red onion (diced)

1 teaspoon of curry powder

4 cups of red leaf (or better still butter lettuce, cut into shreds)

8 flour tortillas

Directions:

1. First, you sauté green and red peppers, onion, garlic and curry powder in a few Tablespoons of water for about 5 minutes.

2. After which you add the chopped vegetables and shredded lettuce, cover, lower heat and steam for about 10 minutes.

3. In the meantime, you warm the tortillas, stove top in a non-stick skillet until pliable or in the microwave wrapped in wet paper.

4. At this point, you spoon about ½ cup of the vegetables in the middle of the warm tortilla.

5. Then you spread about 2 Tablespoons of hummus on one side of the tortilla. (Or, use 1 teaspoon of feta.)

6. Finally, you fold over both sides of the tortilla and then roll.

Mushrooms with Burgundy Sauce Over Polenta

Serves 4

Ingredients:

1 red onion (chopped)

One 15 oz. can diced tomatoes (finely chopped in a blender or food processor)

4 green onions (chopped)

¼ cup of parsley (chopped)

24 oz. of white and baby portabellas mixed mushrooms (sliced)

4 cloves garlic (minced)

2 Tablespoons of Worcestershire sauce

1 cup of red wine

Store-bought pre-made polenta or better still a 3 cups of potenta, prepared:

Directions:

1. First, you sauté onion in water until softened.

2. After which you add garlic and mushrooms and continue to cook until mushrooms are tender and most of the moisture has evaporated.

3. After that, you add tomatoes, Worcestershire sauce, green onions and wine.

4. Then you continue to cook until reduced by about half.

5. At this point, you soften pre-made polenta by warming in the microwave.

6. Furthermore, you add about 1 cup milk or stock and stir to combine until it's about the consistency of mashed potatoes.

7. After that, you add chopped parsley at the last minute.

8. Finally, you serve mushrooms with sauce over softened polenta.

Baked Corn Casserole with Spinach & Chilies

Serves 5-6

Ingredients:

1 cup of cornmeal

¾ cup of milk alternative like almond

2 cans of diced mild chilies

2 ears fresh corn, taken off of cob, or better still pkg frozen, thawed

½ teaspoon of cumin

½ teaspoon of cayenne pepper

One (14-16 oz.) block of firm tofu

1 ½ cup of water

1 pkg of frozen spinach (thawed and water squeezed out)

3 cloves garlic (minced)

1 teaspoon of baking powder

1 teaspoon Salt and Pepper to taste

Condiments: Store-bought Salsa or better still Enchilada sauce

Directions:

1. Meanwhile, you heat oven to 400 degrees

2. After which you prepare cornmeal by heating 1 ½ cup water in a medium saucepan with ½ cup of the milk alternative until almost boiling.

3. After that, you slowly whisk in the corn meal and stir constantly until mixture thickens.

4. Then you transfer to a large bowl.

5. To a food processor, you add the garlic, tofu, 1 cup corn and remaining ¼ cup milk alternative.

6. After which you process until smooth.

7. After that, you stir into the cooked cornmeal in the large bowl.

8. This is when you add the spinach, remaining whole corn, diced chilies, baking powder, spices, salt and pepper and mix well (**NOTE:** This may take some elbow grease).

9. Bake for about 60-70 minutes until crispy and firm at the edges (NOTE: The middle will be a bit wiggly still).

10. At this point, you let stand for about 20-30 minutes before serving.

11. Finally, you serve topped with salsa or enchilada sauce

Baked Tofu

Serves 3

Ingredients:

¼ cup of soy sauce

2 Tablespoons of ketchup

1 dash of hot sauce

¼ teaspoon of ground black pepper

One 16 oz. container firm tofu, drained, halved crosswise and pressed for about 20 minutes to remove some of the water

2 Tablespoons of maple syrup

1 Tablespoon of rice vinegar

¼ teaspoon of garlic powder

Directions:

1. Meanwhile, you heat oven to 375 degrees F.

2. After which you lightly spray a non-stick baking sheet with oil.

3. After that, you slice tofu into 1" cubes.

4. Then in a bowl, stir together the soy sauce, maple syrup, ketchup, vinegar, hot sauce, garlic powder, and black pepper.

5. At this point, you gently stir tofu cubes into sauce.

6. Furthermore, you cover and marinate for at least 5 minutes.

7. After that, you place tofu on the baking sheet in a single layover.

8. Bake for about 15 minutes.

9. Finally, you turn tofu, and bake until it turns golden brown, around 15 minutes more.

Eggplant Szechuan-Style with Peppers & Mushrooms

Serves 4

Ingredients:

1 medium red pepper (cut into 1" cubes)

¼ cup of veggie stock or better still water

1 ½ slice ginger (finely minced)

2 teaspoons of sugar

4 teaspoons of rice vinegar

1 medium eggplant (unpeeled and cut into 1" cubes)

1 pkg of mushrooms (sliced)

1 cloves garlic (finely minced)

2 Tablespoons of soy sauce

1 ½ teaspoons of chili paste

Directions:

1. First, in a small bowl, make broth mixture by adding veggie stock or water, soy sauce, sugar, garlic, ginger, chili paste and vinegar.

2. After which in a large skillet, sauté eggplant in ¼ cup water until soften just a bit and then add peppers and mushrooms and continue to sauté for about 3-4 minutes.

3. After that, you add broth mixture to eggplant, bring to boil and stir.

4. Then you cook for a few minutes until mixture has reduced a little.

5. Finally, you serve over steamed rice.

Pasta with Pesto (No Added Oil)

Serves 4-6

Ingredients:

3 cloves garlic

3 Tablespoons of nutritional yeast

¼ cup of water (more or less depending on desired consistency)

2 cups of tightly packed basil

3 Tablespoons of white or better still red miso

1/8 cup of toasted pine nuts

Directions:

1. First, you blend basil, garlic, miso and pine nuts in food processor.

2. After which you slowly drizzle in water while machine is running to desired consistency.

3. Then you serve over whole wheat spaghetti adding a little pasta water if it becomes too thick.

Chili Topped Potatoes with Corn Salsa

Serves 6

Ingredients:

2 cans (15 oz. each) pinto beans (drained and rinsed)

1 can (about 4 oz.) chopped green chilies

1-2 cloves garlic (crushed or minced)

1 teaspoon of ground cumin

Salt and pepper to taste

6 large russet potatoes

1 cup of salsa Fresca

1 small onion (chopped)

1 teaspoon of chili powder

¼ teaspoon of ground red pepper

Ingredients for the Salsa:

1 tomato (chopped)

1 lime (juiced)

One ear fresh corn on the cop, corn removed and boiled in scant water for about 2 minutes then cooled in the frig

¼ cup of chopped fresh cilantro (divided)

4 scallions, (green and white parts), chopped

Directions:

1. Meanwhile, you heat the oven to 375 degrees.

2. After which you place the potatoes on the rack in the oven and bake for about 45 minutes or until tender.

3. After that, in a saucepan, stir together the beans, salsa, garlic, chili powder, cumin, chilies, onions, red paper and half of the cilantro.

4. At this point, you add salt and pepper to taste.

5. Then you cook over low heat, stirring occasionally, for about 15 minutes.

6. Furthermore, in a separate bowl, stir together the tomato, corn, scallions, remaining cilantro and lime juice.

7. Finally, if you want to serve, I suggest you split potato down the center with a knife and fill with chili.

8. Then you top with corn salsa.

Veggie Tacos

Serves 3

Ingredients:

½ red onion (diced)

½ bell pepper (diced)

3 leaves romaine lettuce (diced)

1/3 cup of hummus recipe

6 corn tortillas

4 oz. of mushrooms (sliced)

1 tomato (diced)

1 avocado (diced)

Ingredients for the salsa

Ingredients for breakfast version: Tofu scramble: ½ block of tofu, crumbled in a town with a fork.

Optional: use broccoli sprouts as a topping or mango chutney as a "salsa"

Salt and pepper

½ teaspoon of turmeric for color

Directions:

1. First, you add red onion, mushrooms and bell pepper to a sauté pan with a little water.

2. After which you sauté until tender.

3. After that, you toast corn tortillas in toaster oven until crisp but pliable.

4. Then you smear a tablespoon or so of hummus on one side of the corn tortilla.

5. This is when you fill the bottom with the veggie mixture.

6. Finally, you top with the tomatoes, lettuce, avocado and salsa.

Directions for Breakfast version:

1. First, you add crumbled tofu to the veggies in the sauté pan along with the turmeric.

2. After which you stir to combine and heat through.

3. After that, you put a small portion into the taco shell and top with remaining ingredients.

Stuffed Peppers

Serves 4-6

Ingredients:

3 red peppers (cut in half lengthwise and seeds removed)

2 cloves garlic (chopped)

8 sun dried tomatoes (soaked in hot water and roughly chopped)

1/3 cup of finely chopped raw cashews

1 ½ cup of cooked rice

1 onion (chopped)

8 oz. mushroom (sliced)

2-3 large leaves Swiss chard (roughly chopped)

1-2 cup of spaghetti sauce or better still tomato sauce

Directions:

1. Meanwhile, you heat oven to 375 degrees.

2. After which you parboil the peppers in boiling water for about 5 minutes. Drain.

Note: feel free to skip this step, but it'll take twice the time to cook in the oven.

3. After that, you allow 40 minutes if you skip this.

4. At this point, you sauté the onions in a large sauté pan with a little water.

5. Then you add garlic and mushrooms and continue to cook until they're almost done.

6. Furthermore, you add the chard and cook until wilted.

7. After that, you add the sun dried tomatoes, the sauce and 1 ½ cups rice.

8. Then you stir to combine.

9. In addition, you fill the peppers "cups" until full and top with chopped cashes.

10. Finally, you cook covered with foil for about 20-25 minutes until heated through.

11. This is when you remove foil and brown cashews for another 5-10 minutes.

Beet, Black Bean Burger

Serves 4

Ingredients:

1 cup of brown rice (cooked)

1/2-3/4 cup of raisins

¾ cup of oats

Salt and pepper (to taste)

1 can black beans (drained)

3 beets, roasted and coarsely chopped (or better still cooked as you like)

1 chipotle in adobo sauce (or better still more if you like it hot)

½ teaspoon of cumin

Directions:

1. First, you put the rice, beets, raisins, chipotle and spices in a food processor and process until well combined.

2. After which you add in the black beans and oats and process a few times until the beans are coarsely chopped.

3. After that, you add more oats if the mixture seems too wet.

4. At this point, you taste for seasons and add more to your liking.

5. This is when you scoop about a cup into your hands and shape it into a patty.

6. Then you pan fry for about 2-3 minutes a side until they have a nice color.

7. Finally, you serve with all of the fixins' - tomato, lettuce, pickles, and onion.

Note: if you want to roast the beets, remove the leaves, and put them on a large piece of aluminum foil.

8. After which you sprinkle with olive oil, salt and pepper and close up the foil.

9. Then you put into a pie tin and roast in a 400-degree oven for about 20-30 minutes.

Thai Coconut Curry Tofu

Serves 4

Ingredients:

½ large onion (coarsely chopped)

1 medium onion (chopped)

1 whole medium red pepper (coarsely chopped)

1 teaspoon of grated ginger

Brown rice or better still quinoa (prepared according to package)

1 container of tofu (drained and cut into 1" squares)

¼ cup of water

½ lb. of green beans (cut into thirds)

1 can of light coconut milk

1 Tablespoons of red curry paste or 2 teaspoons of curry powder

1 teaspoons of salt

Directions:

1. First, dry pan fries the tofu, turning until browned.

2. After which you remove from heat.

3. After that, you heat the ¼ cup water in the pan and sauté the onion until translucent.

4. Then you add the green beans and red pepper and ½ cup water and continue to cook until soft-crisp.

5. At this point, you add the grated ginger, red curry paste or powder and salt to the vegetables.

6. Furthermore, you add the coconut milk and stir.

7. This is when you thin with a little water or veggie stock.

8. After that, you continue to cook until the sauce thickens.

9. Finally, you put the prepared brown rice into a bowl and spoon the vegetable and sauce over.

Direction to Dry Fry:

1. First, you use a nonstick skillet or well-seasoned cast-iron skillet et to medium-low heat.

2. After which you slowly cook the tofu on a dry skillet without oil and press lightly with a spatula to allow the water to evaporate.

3. After that, it will turn a golden yellow color as it cooks.

4. Then when it freely ovens in the pan and is golden brown, flip and cook on the other side.

Tempeh in Hearty Mushroom-Lager Sauce

Ingredients:

Serve 4

1 Tablespoons of soy sauce

1 bunch of asparagus (cut into 1" pieces)

2 ½ cups of lager, such as Samuel Adams

2 green onions (white and free finely sliced)

One 7-oz pkg. tempeh (cut into 1/2" cubes)

10 oz. of cremini mushrooms (sliced)

2 Tablespoons of flour

2 Tablespoons of Dijon mustard

Directions:

1. First, you cook tempeh cubes along with the mushroom for 7-10 minutes, or until browned.

2. After which you add soy sauce and cook two minutes.

3. After that, you transfer tempeh and mushrooms to plate.

4. Then you add asparagus along with ¼ cup water and cover.

5. At this point, you cook until crisp tender and remove to plate.

6. Furthermore, you add 2 Tablespoons of flour to a small container with 2-4 Tablespoons of water, cover and shake.

7. After which you add to the skillet and stir.

8. This is when you cook 1-2 minutes, stirring constantly.

9. In addition, you increase heat and add beer and mustard, and bring mixture to boil.

10. After which you reduce heat to medium-low, and simmer until sauce is thickened.

11. Then you stir in tempeh, asparagus and mushrooms.

12. Finally, you serve over quinoa, rice or mashed potatoes, sprinkled with green onions.

CONCLUSION

Thanks for reading through this book; if you follow judiciously to the recipes outlined above, you will improve your health, fight disease and prolong your life span without effort.

Remember, the only bad action you can take is no action at all.

www.ingramcontent.com/pod-product-compliance
Lightning Source LLC
Chambersburg PA
CBHW081723100526
44591CB00016B/2477